WOMBATS
Burrow Builders

Lynn George

PowerKiDS
press
New York

Published in 2011 by The Rosen Publishing Group, Inc.
29 East 21st Street, New York, NY 10010

First Edition

Editor: Joanne Randolph
Book Design: Kate Laczynski
Photo Researcher: Jessica Gerweck

Photo Credits: Cover, p. 1 Theo Allofs/Getty Images; back cover and interior blueprint © www.iStockphoto.com/Branko Miokovic; pp. 4–5, 6, 8, 16, 18 (wombat, top left), 20, 21, 22 Shutterstock.com; p. 7 Brooke Whatnall/Getty Images; p. 9 © www.iStockphoto.com/Steven Hayes; p. 10 © Biosphoto/Watts Dave/Peter Arnold, Inc.; pp. 11, 14, 15 Jason Edwards/Getty Images; pp. 12–13 Bert and Babs Wells/Getty Images; p. 17 © J. & C. Sohns/age fotostock; p. 18 (hard hat) © www.iStockphoto.com/Don Nichols; pp. 18–19 © Martin Harvey/Peter Arnold, Inc.

Library of Congress Cataloging-in-Publication Data

George, Lynn.
    Wombats : burrow builders / Lynn George — 1st ed.
        p. cm. — (Animal architects)
    Includes index.
    ISBN 978-1-4488-0697-3 (library binding) — ISBN 978-1-4488-1355-1 (pbk.) — ISBN 978-1-4488-1356-8 (6-pack)
    1. Wombats—Habitations—Juvenile literature. I. Title.
    QL737.M39G46 2011
    599.2'4—dc22
                            2010008868

Manufactured in the United States of America

CPSIA Compliance Information: Batch #WS10PK: For Further Information contact Rosen Publishing, New York, New York at 1-800-237-9932

CONTENTS

WHAT IS A WOMBAT?

Have you ever heard of a wombat? It is an Australian **marsupial**, just as koalas and kangaroos are. Wombats have thick, heavy bodies and light brown to black fur. They can run 25 miles per hour (40 km/h) on their short, powerful legs. They have very short tails, big paws with strong claws, large heads, and small eyes. These furry master builders dig **burrows** with their legs, paws, and claws.

Like all marsupials, the mother wombat carries her baby in a pouch. However, a wombat's pouch differs from many other marsupial pouches in one way. The wombat's pouch faces backward to keep dirt from getting in when she digs.

WHICH WOMBAT IS IT?

There are three main **species** of wombats. The common wombat can be 4 feet (1.2 m) long and weigh 77 pounds (35 kg). It has rough fur, a doglike nose, and short, rounded ears.

There are two species of hairy-nosed wombats. If you think their noses might be furry instead of doglike, you would be

Common wombats live along the southeastern coast of Australia and on Tasmania, off Australia's coast. They are also called naked-nosed wombats.

Hairy-nosed wombats have splits in their top lips that let them eat plants that are very close to the ground. Can you see how this wombat's nose differs from the one on the facing page?

right. Both kinds of hairy-nosed wombats have soft fur covering their bodies and long, pointed ears.

Southern hairy-nosed wombats are the smallest wombats. Northern hairy-nosed wombats are the largest ones. They may weigh 88 pounds (40 kg)! They are uncommon, though. Only about 100 are left on Earth.

WHAT WOMBATS DO

Most people sleep at night and are busy during the day. Wombats are different. They are busy at night and sleep during the day.

In cold weather, wombats may come out of their burrows to warm up in the morning or afternoon sun. However, mostly they just come out at night to feed. Each wombat marks

After a cool night, wombats may come out of their burrows to warm up in the morning sun.
Facing page: Though wombats generally come out at night, they may look for food in the early morning or late afternoon, too.

its feeding **territory** with its scent. Wombats eat grasses, leaves, roots, tree bark, moss, and **fungus**. Would you enjoy a wombat's meal?

Wombats like to play. They chase one another and bump one another with their big heads. They even do **somersaults**!

Wombats are marsupials. This means they give birth to babies that have been growing inside their bodies for only a short time. These babies are not fully **developed**. A baby wombat is about the size of a jelly bean when it is born. The hairless baby, or joey, cannot see or hear. It crawls into its mother's pouch and starts drinking her milk. It stays in the

A common wombat and its joey leave their burrow to look for food together.

pouch for a long time while it finishes developing. After six to eight months, it is big enough to leave the pouch for short periods. Soon, it starts to go out at night with its mother.

A wombat joey stays with its mother for two or three years. Then it leaves to dig its own burrow and find a **mate**. It is ready to have babies of its own.

WATCH THAT WOMBAT DIG!

Using only your hands, how fast could you dig a hole big enough to hide in? It would take quite a while, right? Wombats can dig holes for themselves quickly and easily. Their powerful legs, wide paws, and strong claws make them digging machines. If they are in danger, they quickly dig holes and hide inside. In fact, one wombat

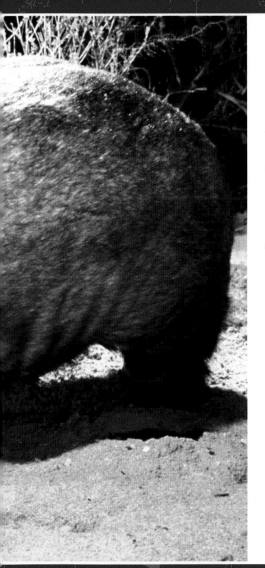

reportedly dug through 6 feet (2 m) of hard soil in just 1 hour! They also use their digging skill to make burrows in which to live.

As wombats dig with their front legs and paws, lots of dirt piles up. To remove it from the burrow, they back out, pushing the dirt behind them. They also use their back legs to push out dirt.

Wombats are so good at digging that they dig many burrows. A common wombat has different kinds of burrows for different purposes. There are short burrows for quick escapes and somewhat longer burrows for resting. There are several large main burrows for living.

This is a northern hairy-nosed wombat tunnel in Australia's Epping National Park. **Facing page:** *Here you can see the opening to a wombat burrow in a grassy field.*

A main burrow may have several openings or only one. The heart of it is the main tunnel. This tunnel may be 11 feet (3 m) below the ground and 100 feet (30 m) long or more.

Side tunnels branch off from the main tunnel. There may be several sleeping rooms. It is like a house!

ONE WOMBAT OR MORE?

You likely live with family members. However, you may know people who live alone. Adult common wombats generally live alone, too. That may sound lonely, but wombats do not seem to mind. When they want company, they visit other wombats, just as you visit friends.

Hairy-nosed wombats are different from common wombats. They are **social**,

which means they like to live near other wombats. These wombats live in **warrens** made up of connected burrows. These are somewhat like the apartment buildings in which some people live. Up to 10 wombats may live in a warren.

Each wombat generally has its own burrow. Females may share a burrow. Males mostly stay alone. However, company is always nearby if a wombat wants it.

INSIDE VIEW:
HAIRY-NOSED
WOMBAT BURROWS

1 Hairy-nosed wombats live in interconnected burrows. The openings to several hairy-nosed wombat burrows may all be in one place. All these openings form a **crater**. The crater may be more than 3 feet (1 m) deep.

8 Each burrow may have up to seven openings. Most burrows have two or three.

7 Sleeping rooms may be at the ends of tunnels or wherever wombats decide to put them. Wombats make nests of grass, leaves, bark, and sticks in the sleeping rooms.

6 The opening leads to the main tunnel. Side tunnels branch off from the main tunnel. There are also tunnels that connect it to neighboring burrows. Together, the connected burrows make up a warren.

2 It is easy to spot the crater. Around it are piles of dirt that may be more than 3 feet (1 m) high and 6 feet (2 m) long.

3 Several trails run in different directions from each burrow opening. They lead to feeding areas and often to other burrows.

4 Hairy-nosed wombats often dig burrows under trees. The roots form the tunnel's roof and guard against it caving in. Wombats spend a lot of time changing or making their burrows longer.

5 The opening to each burrow is just big enough to let the wombat in. It is less than 20 inches (51 cm) wide. That helps keep larger enemies out.

19

BORROWING WOMBAT BURROW

You may be wondering what a wombat does with all its burrows, tunnels, and rooms. A wombat may use different burrows or different parts of a burrow at different times. It cannot use all these places at once. What happens with the unused spaces then?

Other animals **benefit** from the wombat's digging. There are plenty of animals

that like to live underground. Not all of these animals want to dig their own burrows, though. They are happy to use burrows left behind by other animals. Rabbits, foxes, and lizards borrow wombat burrows. Small kangaroos called wallabies do as well. Sometimes these animals turn wombat burrows into their homes. Other times, they simply use them as places to hide from danger or to rest.

BIG TROUBLE FOR WOMBATS

Tens of thousands of wombats once existed. Today the number of these furry builders is falling, and they face many dangers.

People are wombats' main enemy. People have killed them for their fur. People have taken over land where wombats once lived to make farms.

Cows on these farms eat the grass wombats count on for food. There is not enough left for the wombats. Cars sometimes hit wombats and kill them.

There were once other kinds of wombats that became **extinct**. People must take care of the wombats that are still here so they do not become extinct, too.

GLOSSARY

benefit (BEH-neh-fit) To receive use or good from.

burrows (BUR-ohz) Holes animals dig in the ground for shelter.

crater (KRAY-tur) A large hole.

developed (dih-VEH-lupt) Grown up.

extinct (ik-STINGKT) No longer existing.

fungus (FUN-gis) A living thing that is like a plant but that does not have leaves, flowers, or green color and that does not make its own food.

marsupial (mahr-SOO-pee-ul) A type of animal that carries its young in a pouch.

mate (MAYT) A partner for making babies.

social (SOH-shul) Living together in a group.

somersaults (SUH-mer-sawlts) Movements in which a person or animal rolls head over heels.

species (SPEE-sheez) One kind of living thing. All people are one species.

territory (TER-uh-tor-ee) Land or space that an animal guards for its use.

warrens (WAWR-enz) Groups of connected tunnels.

INDEX

WEB SITES

Due to the changing nature of Internet links, PowerKids Press has developed an online list of Web sites related to the subject of this book. This site is updated regularly. Please use this link to access the list:
www.powerkidslinks.com/arch/wombat/